John Stockdale

A Defence of the Rockingham Party

In their Late Coalition with the Right Honourable Frederic Lord North

John Stockdale

A Defence of the Rockingham Party
In their Late Coalition with the Right Honourable Frederic Lord North

ISBN/EAN: 9783337064686

Printed in Europe, USA, Canada, Australia, Japan

Cover: Foto ©ninafisch / pixelio.de

More available books at **www.hansebooks.com**

A DEFENCE OF THE ROCKINGHAM PARTY, &c. &c. &c.

THE present reign will certainly appear to our poſterity full of the nobleſt materials for hiſtory. Many circumſtances ſeem to have pointed it out as a very critical period. The general diffuſion of ſcience has, in ſome degree, enlightened the minds of all men; and has cleared ſuch, as have any influence upon the progreſs of manners and ſociety, from a thouſand unworthy pre-

 poſſeſſions.

poſſeſſions. The diſſipation and luxury that reign uncontrouled have ſpread effiminacy and irreſolution every where.— The grand defection of the United States of America from the mother country, is one of the moſt intereſting events, that has engaged the attention of Europe for centuries. And the number of extraordinary geniuſes that have diſtinguiſhed themſelves in the political world, gives a dignity to the ſcene. They pour a luſtre over the darkeſt parts of the ſtory, and beſtow a beauty upon the tragedy, that it could not otherwiſe have poſſeſſed.

At a time like this, when the attention of mankind has been kept alive by a ſeries of the moſt important events, we ceaſe to admire at things which would otherwiſe appear uncommon, and wonders almoſt loſe their name. Even now, however, when men were almoſt grown callous to novelty, and the youngeſt of us had, like Cato in the play, lived long enough to be " ſurpriſed at nothing," a matter has occurred which few expected, and

and to which, for that reaſon, men of no great ſtrength of mind, of no nerve of political feeling, ſcarcely know how to reconcile themſelves. I refer to the coalition between the friends of the late marquis of Rockingham and the noble commoner in the blue ribbon.

The manner of blaming this action is palpable and eaſy. The cenſure is chiefly directed againſt that wonderful man, whom, at leaſt in their hearts, his countrymen, I believe, have agreed to regard as the perſon of brighteſt genius, and moſt extenſive capacity, that now adorns the Britiſh ſenate. Has not this perſon, we are aſked, for years attacked the noble lord in the moſt unqualified manner? Is there any aſperſion, any inſinuation, that he has not thrown out upon his character? Has he not repreſented him as the weakeſt man, and the worſt miniſter, to whom the direction of affairs was ever committed? Has he not imputed to his prerogative principles, and his palpable miſconduct, the whole catalogue of our misfortunes? If ſuch men as theſe are to unite for the deteſted purpoſes of ambition, what ſecurity can we have for any thing valuable, that yet remains to us? Is not this the very utmoſt reach of frontleſs profligacy? What dependence after this is to be placed in the man, who has thus given the lie to all his profeſſions, and impudently flown in the face of that honeſt and unſuſpecting virtue, which had hitherto given him credit for the rectitude of his intentions?

I do not mean for the preſent to enter into a direct anſwer to theſe ſeveral obſervations. I leave it to others, to reſt the weight of their cauſe upon ſounding exclamations and pompous interogatories. For myſelf, I am firmly perſuaded, that the oftner the late conduct of the Rockingham connexion is ſummoned to the bar of fair reaſon, the more cooly it is conſidered, and the leſs the examiner is led away by the particular prejudices of this ſide or of that, the more commendable it will appear. We do not fear the light.

We do not ſhun the ſcrutiny. We are under no apprehenſions for the conſequences.

I will reſt my argument upon the regular proof of theſe three propoſitions.

Firſt—That the Rockingham connexion, was the only connexion by which the country could be well ſerved.

Secondly—That they were not by themſelves of ſufficient ſtrength to ſupport the weight of adminiſtration.

Thirdly—That they were not the men whoſe ſervices were the moſt likely to be called for by the ſovereign, in the preſent criſis.

Firſt—I am to prove, that the country could not be well ſerved but by the Rockingham connexion.

There are three points principally concerned in the conſtituting a good adminiſtration;

ſtration; liberal principles, reſpectable abilities, and incorruptible integrity.—Let us examine with a view to theſe, the other four parties in the Britiſh government. The connexion of the earl of Shelburne, that of lord North, the Bedford party, and the Scottiſh. In reviewing theſe, it is neceſſary that I ſhould employ a manly freedom, though, at the ſame time, I ſhould be much unwilling to do a partial injuſtice to any of them.

It is true, there is ſome difference between the language of the ſame men in office, and out of office. The Bedford connexion, however, have never been conceived to bear an over favourable aſpect to the cauſe of liberty. They are the avowed enemies of innovation and reform.

The Scottiſh party are pretty much confounded with the ſet of men that are called, by way of diſtinction, the king's friends.

friends. The deſign of theſe men has been to exalt regal power and prerogative upon the ruins of ariſtocracy, and the neck of the people. Arguments, and thoſe by no means of a frivolous deſcription, have been brought to prove, that a moſt ſubtle and deep-laid ſcheme was formed by them, in the beginning of the reign, to ſubſerve this odious purpoſe. It has been ſuppoſed to have been purſued with the moſt inflexible conſtancy, and, like a ſkiff, when it ſails along the meandering courſe of a river, finally to have turned to account the moſt untoward gales.

Lord North, whatever we may ſuppoſe to have been his intrinſic abilities, ſtands forward, as, perhaps, the moſt unfortunate miniſter, that this country ever produced. Misfortune overtook him in the aſſertion of the higheſt monarchical principles. In ſpite of misfortune, he adherred inflexibly to that aſſertion. In the moſt critical ſituations he remained in a ſtate of heſitation and uncertainty, till

till the tide, that "taken at the flood, led up to fortune," was loſt. His verſatility, and the undiſguiſed attachment, that he manifeſted to emolument and power, were ſurely unworthy of the ſtake that was entruſted to him.

In what I have now ſaid, I do not much fear to be contradicted. It was not with a view to ſuch as are attached to any of theſe parties, that I have taken up the pen. Thoſe who come under this deſcription, are almoſt univerſally the advocates of monarchy, and think that they have nothing to regret, but that power and police are not eſtabliſhed upon a more uncontrolable footing among us. To ſuch perſons I do not addreſs myſelf. I know of nothing that the friends of lord Rockingham have to offer that can be of any weight with them; and, for my own part, I ſhould bluſh to ſay a word, that ſhould tend to conciliate their approbation to a ſyſtem, in which my heart was intereſted. The men I wiſh chiefly to have in view, are thoſe that are perſonally attached to the earl of Shelburne; ſuch as ſtand aloof from all parties, and are inclined to have but an indifferent opinion of any; and ſuch as have adhered to the connexion I have undertaken to defend, but whoſe approbation has been ſomewhat cooled by their late conduct. The two laſt in particular, I conſider as leaſt under the power of prejudice, and moſt free to the influence of rational conviction.

The friends of freedom have, I believe, in no inſtance heſitated, but between the Rockingham connexion, and the earl of Shelburne. It is theſe two then that it remains for me to examine. Lord Shelburne had the misfortune of coming very early upon the public ſtage. At that time he connected himſelf with the earl of Bute, and entered with warmth into the oppoſition to Mr. ſecretary Pitt. In this ſyſtem of conduct, however, he did not long perſiſt; he ſpeedily broke with the favourite, and ſoon after joined the celebrated hero, that had lately been the object of his attack. By this person he was introduced to a considerable post in administration. In office, he is chiefly remembered by the very decisive stile of authority and censure he employed, in a public letter, relative to the resistance that was made to the act of 1767, for imposing certain duties in America. From his resignation with lord Chatham, he uniformly and strenuously opposed the measures that were adopted for crushing that resistance. He persevered, with much apparent constancy, in one line of conduct for near ten years, and this is certainly the most plausible period of his story. He first called forth the suspicions of generous and liberal men in every rank of society, by his resolute opposition to the American independency in 1778. But it was in the administration, that seemed to have been formed under so favourable auspices in the spring of 1782, that he came most forward to general examination.

The

The Rockingham connexion, in conformity to what were then ſuppoſed to be the wiſhes of the people, united, though not without ſome heſitation, with the noble earl and his adherents, in the conduct of public affairs. And how did he reward their confidence? He was careful to retain the queſtion reſpecting his real ſentiments upon the buſineſs of America, in as much obſcurity as ever. He wrote officially a letter to ſir Guy Carleton, which has never ſeen the light, by which that officer was induced to declare the American independency already irreverſibly recogniſed by the court of London; by which he appears to have deceived all his brother miniſters without exception; and by which Mr. Fox in particular, was induced to make the ſame declaration with general Carleton to foreign courts, and to come forward in the commons peremptorily to affirm, that there was not a ſecond opinion in the cabinet, upon this intereſting ſubject. How muſt a man of his undiſguiſed and manly character have felt, when, within a week from this time, he found the noble earl declaring that nothing had ever been further from his thoughts, than an unconditional recognition; and successfully exerting himself to bring over a majority in the cabinet to the opposite sentiment? Lord Shelburne's obtaining, or accepting, call it which you will, of the office of first lord of the treasury, upon the demise of lord Rockingham, without the privity of his fellow Ministers, was contrary to every maxim of ingenuous conduct, and every principle upon which an association of parties can be supported. The declaration he made, and which was contradicted both by his own friends in the cabinet, and those of Mr. Fox, that he knew of no reason *in God's earth* for that gentleman's resignation, but that of his having succeeded to the office of premier, was surely sufficiently singular.

But he is celebrated for being a man of large professions, and by these professions he has induced some persons in different classes in society, to esteem him the

the friend of liberty and renovation: What he has held out, however, upon these heads, has not been entirely consistent. He has appeared the enthusiastical partizan of the aristocracy, a kind of government, which, carried to its height, is perhaps, of all the different species of despotism, the most intolerable. He has talked in a very particular stile of his fears of reducing the regal power to a shadow, of his desire that the extension of prerogative should keep pace with the confirmation of popular rights, and his resolution, that, if it were in his power to prevent it, a king of England should never be brought to a level with a king of Mahrattas. The true sons of freedom will not certainly be very apprehensive upon this score, and will leave it to the numbers that will ever remain the adherents of monarchical power, to guard the barriers of the throne. In opposition, his declarations in favour of parliamentary reform seemed indeed very decisive. In administration, he was particularly careful to explain away these

decla-

declarations, and to aſſure the people that he would never employ any influence in ſupport of the meaſure, but would only countenance it ſo far as it appeared to be the ſenſe of parliament. In other words, that he would remain neutral, or at moſt only honour the ſubject with an eloquent harangue, and intereſt himſelf no further reſpecting it.

But let us proceed from his language to his conduct in office. Almoſt every ſalutary meaſure of adminiſtration, from the reſignation of lord North downward, was brought about during the union of the noble earl with the Rockingham connexion. What inference are we to draw from this?—That adminiſtration, as auſpicious as it was tranſitory, has never been charged with more than one error. They were thought too liberal in the diſtribution of two or three ſinecures and penſions. To whom were they diſtributed? Uniformly, excluſively, to the friends of lord Shelburne. Lord Shelburne propoſed them to his auguſt colleague,

colleague, and the marquis, whose faults, if he had any, were an excess of mildness, and an unsuspecting simplicity, perhaps too readily complied. But let it be remembered, that not one of his friends accepted, or to not one of his friends were these emoluments extended. But, if the noble marquis were sparing in the distribution of pensions, the deficiency was abundantly supplied by his successor. While the interests of the people were neglected and forgotten, the attention of the premier was in a considerable degree engrossed by the petty arrangements of office. For one man a certain department of business was marked out; the place had been previously filled by another. Here the first person was at all events to be promoted; and the second gratified with a pension. Thus, in the minute detail of employment, in adjusting the indeclinables of a court calendar, to detach a *commis* from this department, and to fix a clerk in that, burthen after burthen has been heaped upon the shoulders of a callous and lethargic people.—But no

man

man can ſay, that the earl of Shelburne has been idle. Beſide all this, he has reſtored peace to his country. His merits in this buſineſs, have already been ſufficiently agitated. To examine them afreſh would lead me too far from the ſcope of my ſubject. I will not therefore now detain myſelf either to exculpate or criminate the miniſter, to whom, whatever they are, they are principally to be aſcribed.

From the conſiderations already ſuggeſted, I am afraid thus much may be fairly inferred, that the earl of Shelburne is a man, dark, inſidious and inexplicit in his deſigns; no decided friend of the privileges of the people; and in both reſpects a perſon very improper to conduct the affairs of this country. I would hope however, that the celebrated character given of him by the late lord Holland was ſomewhat too ſevere. "I "have met with many, who by perſe- "verance and labour have made them-

"ſelves

" ſelves Jeſuits ; it is peculiar to this man " to have been born one."

Such then is the eſtimate we are compelled to form of a man who in his profeſſions has ſometimes gone as far, as the moſt zealous votaries of liberty. And what is the inference we ſhall draw from this? Shall we, for the ſake of one man ſo ſpecious and plauſible, learn to think the language of all men equally empty and deceitful? Having once been betrayed, ſhall we avoid all future riſk, by treating every pretender to patriotiſm and public ſpirit, as a knave and an impoſtor? This indeed is a concluſion to which the unprincipled and the vicious are ever propenſe. They judge of their fellows by themſelves, and from the depravity of their own hearts are willing to infer, that every honeſty has its price. But the very motive that inclines the depraved to ſuch a mode of reaſoning, muſt, upon the very ſame account, deter the man of virtue from adopting it. Virtue is originally ever ſimple and unſuſpecting.

Conſcious to its own rectitude, and the integrity of its profeſſions, it naturally expects the ſame ſpecies of conduct from others. By every diſappointment of this kind, it is mortified and humbled. Long, very long muſt it have been baffled, and countleſs muſt have been its mortifications, ere it can be induced to adopt a principle of general miſtruſt. And that ſuch a principle ſhould have ſo large a ſpread among perſons, whoſe honeſty, candour forbids us to ſuſpect, is ſurely, of all the paradoxes upon the face of the earth, incomparably the greateſt.—The man of virtue then will be willing, before he gives up all our political connexions without diſtinction, to go along with me to the review of the only one that yet remains to be examined, that of the late marquis of Rockingham.

Too much perhaps cannot be ſaid in their praiſe. They have nearly engroſſed the confidence of every friend of liberty. They are the only men, whoſe principles were never darkened with the cloud of ſuſpicion.

picion. What, let me aſk, has been their uniform conduct during the whole courſe of the reign? They have been ever ſteady in their oppoſition, to whatever bore an ill aſpect to the cauſe of freedom, and to the whole train of thoſe political meaſures, that have terminated in calamity and ruin. They have been twice in adminiſtration. Proſperity and power are uſually circumſtances that prove the ſevereſt virtue. While in power how then did this party conduct themſelves?

Of their firſt adminiſtration the principal meaſure was the ſtamp act. A law that reſtored tranquility to a diſtracted empire. A law, to which, if ſucceeding adminiſtrations had univerſally adhered, we had been at this moment, the excluſive allies and patrons of the whole continent of North America. A law, that they carried in oppoſition to the all-dreaded Mr. Pitt, on the one hand, and on the other, againſt the inclination of thoſe ſecret directors, from whoſe hands they receive their delegated power. They repealed the exciſe upon cyder. They aboliſhed general warrants. And after having been the authors of these and a thousand other benefits in the midst of storms and danger; they quitted their places with a disinterestedness, that no other set of men have imitated. They secured neither place, pension, nor reversion to themselves, or any of their adherents.

Their second administration was indeed very short. But it was crowded with the most salutary measures. The granting a full relief to Ireland. The passing several most important bills of oeconomy and reformation. The passing the contractors bill. The carrying into effect that most valuable measure, the abolishing the vote of custom-house officers in the election of members of parliament. And lastly, the attempt to atchieve, that most important of all objects, the establishment of an equal representation. What might not have been expected from their longer continuance in office?

But I will not confine myſelf to the conſideration of their conduct as a body. The characters of the individuals of which they are compoſed, will ſtill further illuſtrate their true principles, and furniſh a ſtrong additional recommendation of them, to every friend of virtue and of liberty. That I may not overcharge this part of my ſubject, I will only mention two or three of their moſt diſtinguiſhed leaders.

The character of the preſent chancellor of the exchequer is entirely an *unique*. Though mixing in all the buſy ſcenes of life, though occupying for many years a principal place in the political affairs of this country, he has *kept himſelf unſpotted from the world*.—The word of the elder Cato was eſteemed ſo ſacred with the Romans, that it became a proverb among them reſpecting things, ſo improbable, that their truth could not be eſtabliſhed even by the higheſt authority, " I would " not believe it, though it were told me " by Cato." And in an age much more diſſipated,

diſſipated than that of Cato, the integrity and honour of the noble lord I have mentioned, has become equally proverbial. Not bonds, nor deeds, nor all the ſhackles of law, are half ſo much to be depended upon as is his lighteſt word. He is deaf to all the prejudices of blood or private friendſhip, and has no feelings but for his country.

Of the duke of Portland, I can ſay the leſs, as not having had an opportunity of knowing much reſpecting him. His candour and his honour have never been queſtioned. And I remember, in the debate upon the celebrated ſeceſſion of the Rockingham party, upon the death of their leader, to have heard his abilities particularly vouched in very ſtrong terms, by Mr. chancellor Pitt, and the preſent lord Sidney. The latter in particular, though one of my lord Shelburne's ſecretaries of ſtate, fairly avowed in ſo many words, that he ſhould have been better ſatisfied with the appointment of his grace, to the office he now holds, than

than he was, with the noble lord, under whom he acted.

The character of lord Keppel, with persons not attached to any party, has usually been that of a man of much honesty and simplicity, without any remarkable abilities. It is a little extraordinary however, that, though forced by a combination of unfavourable circumstances into a public speaker, he is yet, even in that line, very far from contempt. His speeches are manly, regular, and to the purpose. His defence upon his trial at Portsmouth, in which he must naturally be supposed to have had at least a principal share, has, in my opinion, much beauty of composition. The adversaries of this party, though unwilling to admit that the navy was so much improved under his auspices as was asserted, have yet, I believe, universally acknowledged his particular activity and diligence.

But

But I come to the great boaſt of his own party, and the principal object of attack to their enemies, the celebrated Mr. Fox. Men of formality and ſanctity have complained of him as diſſipated. They do not pretend however to aggravate their accuſation, by laying to his charge any of the greater vices. His contempt of money, and his unbounded generoſity, are univerſally confeſſed. Let ſuch then know, that diſſipation, ſo qualified, is a very ſlight accuſation againſt a public man, if indeed it deſerves a ſerious conſideration. In all expanſive minds, in minds formed for an extenſive ſtage, to embrace the welfare and the intereſt of nations, there is a certain inceſſant activity, a principle that muſt be employed. Debar them from their proper field, and it will moſt inevitably run out into exceſſes, which perhaps had better have been avoided. But do theſe excreſcences, which only proceed from the richneſs and fertility of the ſoil, diſqualify a man for public buſineſs? Far, very far from it. Where ever was there a man, who pushed dissipation and debauchery to a greater length, than my lord Bolingbroke? And yet it is perhaps difficult to say, whether there ever existed a more industrious, or an abler minister. The peace of Utrecht, concluded amidst a thousand difficulties, from our allies abroad, and our parties, that were never so much exasperated against each other at home; must ever remain the monument of his glory. His opposition to sir Robert Walpole seems evidently to have been founded npon the most generous principles. And though the warmth and ebullition of his passions evermore broke in upon his happiest attempts, yet were his exertions in both instances attended with the most salutary consequences. But Mr. Fox appears to me to possess all the excellencies, without any any of the defects of lord Bolingbroke. His passions have, I believe, never been suspected of having embroiled the affairs of his party, and he has uniformly retained the confidence of them all. His friendships have been solid and unſhaken. His conduct cool and intrepid. The littleneſs of jealouſy never diſcoloured a conception of his heart. In office he was more conſtant and indefatigable, than lord Bolingbroke himſelf. All his leſſer purſuits ſeemed annihilated, and he was ſwallowed up in the direction of public affairs.

He has been accuſed of ambition. Ambition is a very ambiguous term. In its loweſt ſenſe, it ſinks the meaneſt, and degrades the dirtieſt of our race. In its higheſt, I cannot agree with thoſe who ſtile it the defect of noble minds. I eſteem it worthy of the loudeſt commendation, and the moſt aſſiduous culture. Mr. Fox's is certainly not an ambition of emolument. Nobody dreams it. It is not an ambition, that can be gratified by the diſtribution of places and penſions. This is a paſſion, that can only dwell in the weakeſt and moſt imbecil minds. Its neceſſary concomitants, are official inattention and oſcitancy. No. The ambition of this hero is a ge-

nerous

nerous thirſt of fame, and a deſire of poſ-ſeſſing the opportunity of conferring the moſt laſting benefits upon his country. It is an inſtinct, that carries a man for-ward into the field of fitneſs, and of God.

The vulgar, incapable of comprehend-ing theſe exalted paſſions, are apt upon the ſlighteſt occaſions to ſuſpect, that this heroical language is only held out to them for a lure, and that the moſt illuſtrious characters among us are really governed by paſſions, equally incident to the meaneſt of mankind. Let ſuch ex-amine the features and the manners of Mr. Fox. Was that man made for a Jeſuit? Is he capable of the dirty, la-borious, inſidious tricks of a hypocrite? Is there not a certain manlineſs about him, that diſdains to miſlead? Are not candour and ſincerity, bluntneſs of man-ner, and an unſtudied air, conſpicuous in all he does?— I know not how far the argument may go with others, with me, I confeſs, it has much weight. I believe a man of ſterling genius, incapable of the littleneſſes and meanneſſes, incident to the vulgar courtier. What are the principal characteriſtics of genius? Are they not large views, infinite conceptions, a certain manlineſs and intrepidity of thinking? But all real and ſerious vice originates in ſelfiſh views, narrow conceptions, and intellectual cowardice. A man of genius may poſſibly be thoughtleſs, diſſipated and unſtudied; but he cannot avoid being conſtant, generous, and ſincere. The union of firſt rate abilities with malignity, avarice, and envy, ſeems to me very nearly as incredible a phenomenon, as a mermaid, a unicorn, or a phœnix.

I cannot overcome the propenſity I feel to add Mr. Burke to this illuſtrious catalogue, though the name of this gentleman leads me out of the circle of the cabinet. Mr. Burke raiſed himſelf from an obſcure ſituation, by the greatneſs of his abilities, and his unrivalled genius. Never was diſtinction more nobly earned.

Of

Of every ſpecies of literary compoſition he is equally a maſter. He excels alike in the moſt abſtruſe metaphyſical diſquiſition, and in the warmeſt and moſt ſpirited painting. His rhetoric is at once ornamented and ſublime. His ſatire is poliſhed and ſevere. His wit is truly Attic. Luxuriant in the extreme, his alluſions are always ſtriking, and always happy. But to enumerate his talents, is to tell but half his praiſe. The application he has made of them is infinitely more to his honour. He has devoted himſelf for his country. The drieſt and moſt laborious inveſtigations have not deterred him. Among a thouſand other articles, that might be mentioned, his ſyſtem of œconomical reform muſt for ever ſtand forth, alike the monument of his abilities, and his patriotiſm. His perſonal character is of the moſt amiable kind. Humanity and benevolence are ſtrongly painted in his countenance. His tranſactions with lord Rockingham were in the higheſt degree honourable to him. And the more they are inveſtigated, and the better they are un-

understood, the more disinterestedness of virtue, and generous singularity of thinking, will be found to have been exhibited on both sides.

It is necessary perhaps, that I should say a word respecting the aristocratical principles of this gentleman, by which he is distinguished from the rest of his party. To these principles I profess myself an enemy. I am sorry they should be entertained by a person, for whom, in every other respect, I feel the highest veneration. But the views of that man must be truly narrow, who will give up the character of another, the moment he differs from him in any of his principles. I am sure Mr. Burke is perfectly sincere in his persuasion. And I hope I have long since learned not to question the integrity of any man, upon account of his tenets, whether in religion or politics, be they what they may. I rejoice however, that this gentleman has connected himself with a set of men, by the rectitude of whose views, I trust, the ill tendency of any such involuntary error will be effectually counteracted. In the mean time this deviation of Mr. Burke from the general principles of his connexion, has given occasion to some to impute aristocratical views to the whole party The best answer to this, is, that the parliamenty reform was expresly stipulated by lord Rockingham, in his coalition with the earl of Shelburne, as one of the principles, upon which the Administration of March, 1782, was formed.

From what has been said, I consider my first proposition as completely established, that the Rockingham party was the only connexion of men, by which the country could be well served.

I would however just observe one thing by the way. I forsee that my first proposition lies open to a superficial and childish kind of ridicule. But in order to its operation, it is not necessary to say, that the friends of lord Rockingham were persuaded, that the country could

not

not be well ſerved, but by themſelves. In reality, this is the proper and philoſophical ſtate of it: that each individual of that connexion was perſuaded, that the country could not be well ſerved but by his friends. And I truſt, it has now appeared, that this was a juſt and rational perſuaſion.

The next argument adduced in confirmation of my theſis, is, that they were not by themſelves of ſufficient ſtrength, to ſupport the weight of adminiſtration. It is certainly a melancholy conſideration, that there ſhould not be virtue enough left in a people to ſupport an adminiſtration of honeſt views and uniform principles, againſt all the cabals of faction. This however, is incontrovertibly the caſe with Britain. The bulk of her inhabitants are become, in a very high degree, inattentive, and indifferent to the conduct of her political affairs. This has been, at one time, aſcribed to their deſpair of the commonwealth, and their mortification in per-

perceiving a certain courſe of mal-adminiſtration perſiſted in, in defiance of the known ſenſe of the country. At another time, it has been imputed to their experience of the hollowneſs of all our public pretenders to patriotiſm. I am afraid, the cauſe is to be ſought in ſomething, more uniform in it's operation, and leſs honourable to the lower ranks of ſociety, than either of theſe. In a word, luxury and diſſipation have every where looſened the bands of political union. The intereſt of the public has been forgotten by all men; and we have been taught to laugh at the principles, by which the patriots of former ages were induced, to ſacrifice their fortunes and their lives for the welfare of their citizens. Provided the cup of enjoyment be not daſhed from our own lips, and the pillow of ſloth torn away from our own heads, we do not aſk, what ſhall be the fate of our liberties, our poſterity, and our country. Diſintereſted affection ſeems to have taken up her laſt refuge in a few choice ſpirits, and elevated minds, who appear among us, like the inhabitants of another world. In the mean time, while the lower people have been *careful for none of these things*, they have been almost constantly decided in the senate, not by a view to their intrinsic merits, but in conformity to the jarring interests, and the inexplicable cabals of faction. In such a situation, alas! what can unprotected virtue do? Destitute of all that comeliness that allures; stripped of that influence that gives weight and consideration; and unskilled in the acts of intrigue?

In conformity to these ideas, when the choice of an administration was once again thrown back upon the people, in March, 1782, we perceive, that no one party found themselves sufficiently strong for the support of government; and a coalition became necessary between the Rockingham connexion, and a person they never cordially approved, the earl of Shelburne. Even thus supported, and called to the helm, with perhaps as much popularity, as any administration ever enjoyed,

joyed, they did not carry their meaſure in parliament without difficulty. The inconſiderate and intereſted did even think proper to ridicule their imbecility; particularly in the houſe of lords. The moſt unſuſpected of all our patriots, Mr. Burke, was reduced to the neceſſity of ſo far contracting his ſyſtem of reform upon this account, as to have afforded a handle to ſuperficial raillery and abuſe.

But turn we to the adminiſtration that ſucceeded them; who ſtill retained ſome pretenſions to public ſpirit; and among whom there remained ſeveral individuals, whoſe claim to political integrity was indiſputably. Weaker than the miniſtry of lord Rockingham, to what ſhifts were they not reduced to preſerve their precarious power? Theſe are the men, who have been loudeſt in their cenſures of the late coalition. And yet did not they form coalitions, equally extraordinary with that which is now under conſideration? To omit the noble lord who preſided at the treaſury board, and to confine myſelf to thoſe inſtances, which Mr. Fox had occaſion to mention in treating my ſubject. Was there not the late chancellor of the exchequer, who has been ſevereſt in his cenſures of lord North, and the lord advocate of Scotland, who was his principal ſupporter, and was for puſhing the American meaſures, even to greater lengths, than the noble patron himſelf? Was there not the maſter general of the ordnance, who has ever gone fartheſt in his view of political reform, and declaimed moſt warmly againſt ſecret influence; and the lord chancellor, the moſt determined enemy of reform, and who has been ſuppoſed the principal vehicle of that influence? Laſtly, was there not, in the ſame manner, the ſecretary of ſtate for the home department, who was moſt unwearied in his invectives againſt lord Bute; and the right honourable Mr. Jenkinſon, who has been conſidered by the believers in the inviſible power of that nobleman, as the chief inſtrument of his deſigns.

With

With theſe examples of the neceſſity of powerful ſupport and extenſive combination, what mode of conduct was it, that it was moſt natural, moſt virtuous, and moſt wiſe, for the Rockingham connexion to adopt? I confeſs, I can perceive none more obvious, or more juſt, than that which they actually adopted, a junction with the noble commoner in the blue ribbon. At leaſt, from what has been ſaid, I truſt, thus much is evident beyond control, that they had juſt reaſon to conſider themſelves abſtractedly, as too weak for the ſupport of government.

Still further to ſtrengthen my argument, I affirm, in the third place, that they were not the men, whoſe ſervices were likely to be called for by the Sovereign. I believe, that this propoſition will not be thought to ſtand in need of any very abſtruſe train of reaſoning to ſupport it. The late events reſpecting it have been, inſtead of a thouſand arguments. From an apprehenſion, probably, of the uncourtierlineſs of their temper,

and

and their inflexible attachment to a ſyſtem; it ſeems to appear by thoſe events, that the ſovereign had contracted a ſort of backwardneſs to admit them into his councils, which it is to be hoped, was only temporary. It was however ſuch, as, without any other apparent cauſe to cooperate with it, alone ſufficed to delay the forming an adminiſtration for ſix weeks, in a moſt delicate and critical juncture. Even the union of that noble perſon, who had been conſidered as his majeſty's favourite miniſter, did not appear to be enough to ſubdue the averſeneſs. However then we may hope, that untainted virtue and ſuperior abilities, when more intimately known, may be found calculated to ſurmount prejudices and conciliate affection; it ſeems but too evident, that in the critical moment, thoſe men, by whom alone we have endeavoured to prove, that the country could be well ſerved, would not voluntarily have been thought on.

But it does not ſeem to have been enough conſidered, at what time the coalition was made. The Rockingham connexion, along with thouſands of their fellow citizens, who were unconnected with any party, were induced, from the pureſt views, to diſapprove of the late treaty of peace. The voting with the friends of lord North upon that queſtion, was a matter purely incidental. By that vote however, in which a majority of the commons houſe of parliament was included, the adminiſtration of lord Shelburne was diſſolved. It was not till after the diſſolution was really effected, that the coalition took place. In this ſituation ſomething was neceſſary to be done. The nation was actually without a miniſtry. It was a criſis that did not admit of heſitation and delay. The country muſt, if a ſyſtem of delay had been adopted, have immediately been thrown back into the hands of thoſe men, from whom it had been ſo laboriouſly forced ſcarce twelve months before; or it muſt have been committed to the conduct of perſons even leſs propitious to the cauſe of liberty, and the privileges of the people. A ſituation, like this, called for a firm and manly conduct. It was no longer a time to ſtoop to the yoke of prejudice. It was a time, to burſt forth into untrodden paths; to loſe ſight of the heſitating and timid; and generouſly to adventure upon a ſtep, that ſhould rather have in view ſubſtantial ſervice, than momentary applauſe; and ſhould appeal from the ſhort-ſighted deciſion of ſyſtematic prudence, to the tribunal of facts, and the judgment of poſterity.

But why did I talk of the tribunal of facts? Events are not within the diſpoſi- of human power. "'Tis not in mortals "to command ſucceſs." And the characters of wiſdom and virtue, are therefore very properly conſidered by all men, who pretend to ſober reflection, as independent of it. If then, as I firmly believe, the coalition was founded in the wiſeſt and moſt generous views, the man, that values himſelf upon his rational nature, will

will not wait for the event. He will immediately and peremptorily decide in its favour. Though it ſhould be annihilated to-morrow; though it had been originally fruſtrated in its views, reſpecting the continuation of a miniſtry; he would not heſitate to pronounce, that it was formed in the moſt expanſive and long-ſighted policy, in the nobleſt and moſt prudent daring, in the warmeſt generoſity, and the trueſt patriotiſm.

But it will be ſaid, a coalition of parties may indeed be allowed to be in many caſes proper and wiſe; but a coalition between parties who have long treated each other with the extremeſt rancour, appears a ſpecies of conduct, abhorrent to the unadulterated judgment, and all the native prepoſſeſſions of mankind. It plucks away the very root of unſuſpecting confidence, and can be productive of nothing, but anarchy and confuſion.

In anſwer to this argument, I will not cite the happy effects of the coalition between parties juſt as oppoſite, by which Mr. Pitt was introduced into office in the cloſe of a former reign. Still leſs will I cite the coalition of the earl of Shelburne, with ſeveral leaders of the Bedford connexion, and others, whoſe principles were at leaſt as inimical to the popular cauſe, and the parliamentary reform, as thoſe of Lord North; and the known readineſs of him and his friends to have formed a junction with the whole of that connexion. I need not even hint at the probability there exiſts, that the noble lord then in adminiſtration, would have been happy to have formed the very coalition himſelf, which he is willing we ſhould ſo much reprobate in another. I need not mention the ſuſpicions, that naturally ſuggeſted themſelves upon the invincible ſilence of his party, reſpecting the maladminiſtration of lord North, for ſo long a time; and their bringing forward the ſingular charge of fifty unaccounted millions at the very moment that the coalition was completed. I ſhould be ſorry to have it ſuppoſed, that the connexion

I am

I am defending, ever took an example from the late premier, for one article of their conduct. And I think the mode of vindicating them, not from temporary examples, but from eternal reason, as it is in itself most striking and most honourable, so is it not a whit less easy and obvious.

Let it be remembered then, in the first place, that there was no other connexion, sufficiently unquestionable in their sincerity, and of sufficient weight in the senate, with which to form a coalition. The Bedford party, had they even been willing to have taken this step in conjunction with the friends of lord Rockingham, were already stripped of some of their principal and ablest members, by the arts of lord Shelburne. Whether these ought to be considered in sound reason, as more or less obnoxious than lord North, I will not take upon me to determine. Certain I am, that the Scottish connexion were, of all others, the most suspicious in themselves, and the most odious to the people. The only choice then that remained, was that which was made. The only ſubject for deliberation, was, whether this choice were more or leſs laudable than, on the other hand, the deſerting entirely the intereſts of their country, and leaving the veſſel of the ſtate to the mercy of the winds.

Secondly, I would obſerve that the principal ground of diſpute between lord North and his preſent colleagues in adminiſtration, was done away by the termination of the American war. An impeachment of the noble lord for his paſt errors was perfectly out of the queſtion. No one was mad enough to expect it. A vein of public ſpirit, diffuſing itſelf among all ranks of ſociety, is the indiſpenſible concomitant of impeachments and attainder. And ſuch a temper, I apprehend, will not be ſuſpected to be characteriſtic of the age in which we live. But were it otherwiſe, the Rockingham connexion certainly never ſtood in the way of an impeachment, had it been meditated.

tated. And, exclusive of this question, I know of no objection, that applies particular to the noble lord, in contradistinction to any of the other parties into which we are divided.

But, in the third place, the terms upon which the coalition was made, form a most important article of consideration in estimating its merits. They are generally understood to have been these two; that the Rockingham connexion should at all times have a majority in the cabinet; and that lord North should be be removed to that "hospital of incurables," as lord Chesterfield has stiled it, the house of lords. Surely these articles are the happiest that could have been conceived for preserving the power of administration, as much as may be, with the friends of the people. Places, merely of emolument and magnificence, must be bestowed somewhere. Where then can they be more properly lodged, than in the hands of those who are best able to support a liberal and virtuous administration?

I beg leave to add once more, in the fourth place, that, whatever the demerits of lord North as a minifter may be fuppofed to have been, he is perhaps, in a thoufand other refpects, the fitteft man in the world to occupy the fecond place in a junction of this fort. The union of the Rockingham connexion with the earl of Shelburne laft year, was, I will admit, lefs calculated to excite popular aftonifhment, and popular difapprobation, than the prefent. In the eye of cool reafon and fober forefight, I am apt to believe, it was much lefs wife and commendable. Lord Shelburne, though he has been able to win over the good opinion of feveral, under the notion of his being a friend of liberty, is really, in many refpects, ftiffly ariftocratical, or highly monarchical. Lord Shelburne is a man of infatiable ambition, and who purfues the ends of that ambition by ways the moft complex and infidious. The creed of lord North, whatever it may be, upon general political queftions, is confiftent and intelligible. For my own part, I do not believe him to be ambitious.

It

It is not poſſible, with his indolent and eaſy temper, that he ſhould be very ſuſceptible to ſo reſtleſs a paſſion. In the heroical ſenſe of that word, he ſits looſe to fame. He is undoubtedly deſirous, by all the methods that appear to him honourable and juſt, to enrich and elevate his family. He wiſhes to have it in his power to oblige and to ſerve his friends. But I am exceedingly miſtaken, if he entered into the preſent alliance from views of authority and power. Upon the conditions I have mentioned, it was a ſcheme, congenial only to a man of a dark and plotting temper. But the temper of lord North is in the higheſt degree candid, open and undiſguiſed. Eaſy at home upon every occaſion, there is not a circle in the world to which his preſence would not be an addition. It is calculated to inſpire unconſtraint and confidence into every breaſt. Simple and amiable is the juſt deſcription of his character in every domeſtic relation; conſtant and unreſerved in his connexions of friendſhip. The very verſatility and pliableneſs, ſo loudly con-

demned

demned in his former situation, is now an additional recommendation. Is this the man, for whose intrigues and conspiracies we are bid to tremble?

Another charge that has been urged against the coalition, is, that it was a step that dictated to the sovereign, and excluded all, but one particular set of men, from the national councils. The first part of this charge is somewhat delicate in its nature. I shall only say respecting it, that, if, as we have endeavoured to prove, there were but one connexion, by which the business of administration could be happily discharged, the friend of liberty, rejoicing in the auspicious event, will not be very inquisitive in respect to the etiquette, with which they were introduced into the government. In the mean time, far from intending an exclusion, they declared publicly, that they would be happy to receive into their body any man of known integrity and abilities, from whatever party he came. The declaration has never been contradicted.—

Strangers

Strangers to the remoteſt idea of proſcription, they erected a fortreſs, where every virtue, and every excellence might find a place.

The only remaining objection to the coalition that I know of, that it ſhocks eſtabliſhed opinions, is not, I think, in itſelf, calculated to have much weight, and has, perhaps, been ſufficiently animadverted upon, as we went along, in what has been already ſaid. The proper queſtion is, was it a neceſſary ſtep? Was there any other way, by which the country could be redeemed? If a ſatisfactory anſwer has been furniſhed to theſe enquiries, the inevitable concluſion in my opinion is, that the more it ſhocked eſtabliſhed opinions, and the more intellectual nerve it demanded, the more merit did it poſſeſs, and the louder applauſe is its due.

I am not inclined to believe, that a majority of my countrymen, upon reflection, have diſapproved this meaſure. I am happy to perceive, that ſo much of that good ſenſe and manly thinking in public queſtions, that has for ages been conſidered as the characteriſtic quality of Engliſhmen, is ſtill left among us. There can be nothing more honourable than this.—By it our commonalty, though unable indeed to foreſtal the hero and the man of genius in his ſchemes, do yet, if I may be allowed the expreſſion, tread upon his heels, and are prepared to follow him in all his views, and to glow with all his ſentiments.

Senſible however, that in the firſt bluſh of ſuch a ſcheme, its enemies muſt neceſſarily find their advantage in entrenching themſelves behind thoſe prejudices, that could not be eradicated in a moment, I was willing to wait for the hour of calmneſs and deliberation. I reſolved cooly to let the firſt guſt of prepoſſeſſion blow over, and the ſpring tide of cenſure exhauſt itſelf. I believed, that ſuch a cauſe demanded only a fair and candid hearing.

hearing. I have endeavoured to difcharge my part in obtaining for it fuch a hearing. And I muft leave the reft to my readers.

Among thefe there probably will be fome, who, ftruck with the force of the arguments I have adduced on the one hand, and entangled in their favourite prejudices on the other, will remain in a kind of fufpence; afhamed to retract their former opinions, but too honeft to deny all weight and confideration to thofe I have defended. To thefe I have one word to fay, and with that one word I will conclude. I will fuppofe you to confefs, that appearances, exclufive of the controverted ftep, are in a thoufand inftances favourable to the new minifters. They have made the ftrongeft profeffions, and the largeft promifes of attachment to the general caufe. To profeffions and promifes I do not wifh you to truft. I fhould blufh to revive the odious and exploded maxim, not men, but meafures. If you cannot place ſome confidence in the preſent adminiſtration, I adviſe you, as honeſt men, to do every thing in your power to drive them from the helm. But you will hardly deny, that all their former conduct has afforded reaſons for confidence. You are ready to admit, that, in no inſtance, but one, have they committed their characters. In that one inſtance, they have much to ſay for themſelves, and it appears, at leaſt, very poſſible, that they may have been acted in it, by virtuous and generous principles, even though we ſhould ſuppoſe them miſtaken. Remember then, that popularity and fame are the very nutriment of virtue. A thirſt for fame is not a weakneſs. It is "the noble mind's diſtinguiſhing perfection." If then you would bind adminiſtration by tenfold ties to the cauſe of liberty, do not withdraw from them your approbation till they have forfeited it, by betraying, in one plain and palpable inſtance, the principles upon which they have formerly acted. I believe they need no new bonds, but are un-

changeably

changeably fixed in the generous system, with which they commenced. But thus much is certain. If any thing can detach them from this glorious cause; if any thing can cool their ardour for the common weal, there is nothing that has half so great a tendency to effect this, as unmerited obloquy and disgrace.

F I N I S.

www.ingramcontent.com/pod-product-compliance
Lightning Source LLC
Chambersburg PA
CBHW031759090426
42739CB00008B/1082

9783337064686